The Cat's MEOW

Greer Lawrence

WITH ILLUSTRATIONS BY
Patricia Shea

SMITHMARK

Dedication
In Memory of Patsy Shea

Acknowledgments

My thanks to all the following cats and their people—

Brewster, Whiskers and Barbara, Catherine, Elizabeth, Patrick and Cecilia Bauer

Fred, Wilma and Howard Finkle

Molly, Eddie and Rob and Dina Fograshy

Noel, Spot and Jenn Kerns

Jacobi Wan, Maya and Elizabeth Loonan

Max, Murphy, Missy and Cree Maxson and Ernest Brandt

Dali, Zelda and Carol Rainey and Bud Hopkins

Ricky, Jones, LC, IV and Antonio M. Rosario

Sly and Kristin Soltis

Isis, Thomas and Ellen Waters-Thomas

—PATRICIA SHEA

This edition published in 1997 by SMITHMARK Publishers, a division of U.S. Media Holdings, Inc., 16 East 32nd Street, New York, NY 10016.

SMITHMARK books are available for bulk purchase for sales promotion and premium use. For details write or call the manager of special sales, SMITHMARK Publishers, 16 East 32nd Street, New York, NY 10016; (212) 532-6600.

This book was designed and produced by Todtri Productions Limited P.O. Box 572, New York, NY 10116-0572 FAX: (212) 279-1241

Printed and bound in Singapore

Library of Congress Catalog Card Number 96-71468
ISBN 0-7651-9427-9

Author: Greer Lawrence
Illustrator: Patricia Shea

Publisher: Robert M. Tod
Editorial Director: Elizabeth Loonan
Senior Editor: Cynthia Sternau
Production Coordinator: Annie Kaufmann
Designer: Jacquerie Productions

If a fish is the movement of water embodied,
given shape, then a cat is a diagram
and pattern of subtle air.

—DORIS LESSING

On Feline Inspiration

Great artists are drawn to cats as much as cats are drawn to milk. Whether immortalized in the tombs of Egypt, the scrolls of Japan, the statuary of ancient Greece, or illuminated medieval manuscripts, the cat has sparked the imagination of countless artists throughout history. The antics of the domestic feline have been captured by such painters as William Hogarth, Marc Chagall, James McNeill Whistler, Pablo Picasso, and Leonardo da Vinci. Gottfried Mind painted his way to fame and fortune with his cat Minette on his lap, and became known as the "Raphael of the cat world." Louis Wain discovered his calling in life when so utterly charmed by Peter, his black-and-white cat, that he felt compelled to paint his first feline portrait.

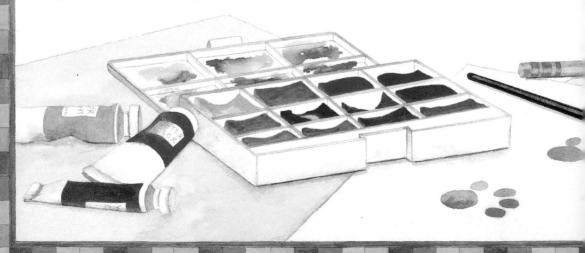

The Well-Read Cat

Many a writer has drawn inspiration from a feline friend as well. Edgar Allan Poe often wrote with his Catterina sitting on his shoulders, and Ernest Hemingway had, at one time, thirty cats. Charles Baudelaire was so devoted a lover of cats that he could never see one without picking it up to caress and talk to it. A little gray Persian gave solace to Thomas Hardy in his last years, mysteriously vanishing when his master died. Just as cats have inspired the work of so many brilliant authors, so too have they inspired their owners to give them suitably eloquent names.

WHAT'S IN A NAME?

Robert Southey bestowed a truly regal title on his favorite feline: The most Noble the Archduke Rumpelstiltzchen, Marquis Macbum, Earl Tomlemagne, Baron Raticide, Waowhler, and Skaratch (a.k.a. Rumpel). Other writers, however, chose simpler but no less inventive names. Among Théophile Gautier's feline companions were Don Pierrot de Navarre, Seraphita, and their offspring Enjolras, Gavroche, and Eponine, named after characters from Victor Hugo's *Les Misérables*. Mark Twain selected cat names that were difficult to pronounce, such as Apollinaris, Beelzebub, Blatherskite, and Zoroaster, ostensibly to serve as elocution lessons for his children. And T. S. Eliot, possibly the most renowned of all cat lovers, kept company with George Pushdragon, Pattipaws, and Wiscus, among others.

When my cat and I entertain each other with mutual antics, as playing with a garter, who knows but that I make more sport for her than she makes for me? Shall I conclude her to be simple that has her time to begin or to refuse to play, as freely as I have mine. Nay, who knows but that it is a defect of my not understanding her language (for doubtless cats can talk and reason with one another) that we agree no better; and who knows but that she pities me for being no wiser than to play with her; and laughs, and censures my folly in making sport for her, when we two play together.

—MICHEL DE MONTAIGNE

Whether in play or in earnest,
cats are the very embodiment of elegance.

—CHARLES H. ROSS

*T*he playful kitten, with its pretty little tigerish gambols, is infinitely more amusing than half the people one is obliged to live with in the world.

—LADY SYDNEY MORGAN

Animals are such agreeable friends—they ask no

questions; they pass no criticisms.

—GEORGE ELIOT

*C*ats do not need to be shown how to have a good time, for they are unfailingly ingenious in that respect.

—JAMES MASON

*T*wo cats sat on a garden wall,
For an hour or so together;
First they talked about nothing at all,
And then they talked of the weather.

—D'ARCY WENTWORTH THOMPSON

A cat improves the garden wall in sunshine,
and the hearth in foul weather.

—JUDITH MERKLE RILEY

Like a graceful vase, a cat,

even when motionless, seems to flow.

—GEORGE F. WILL

A cat may go to a monastery, but she still remains a cat.

ETHIOPIAN PROVERB

The cat loves fish, but hates wet feet.

ITALIAN PROVERB

*I*t is a brave bird that makes its nest in the cat's ear.

HINDI PROVERB

A cat bitten once by a snake dreads even rope.

ARABIC PROVERB

He who is a little cat outside is a little dog at home.

ESTONIAN PROVERB

Happy owner, happy cat. Indifferent owner, reclusive cat.

CHINESE PROVERB

The cat knows whose lips she licks.

LATIN PROVERB

The cat is a lion in a jungle of small bushes.

ENGLISH PROVERB

The Sphinx

In a dim corner of my room
   For longer than my fancy thinks
   A beautiful and silent Sphinx
Has watched me through the shifting gloom.

Dawn follows Dawn and Nights grow old
   And all the while this curious cat
   Lies couching on the Chinese mat
With eyes of satin rimmed with gold.

Upon the mat she lies and leers,
   And on the tawny throat of her
   Flutters the soft and silky fur
Or ripples to her pointed ears.

Come forth, my lovely seneschal!
   So somnolent, so statuesque!
   Come forth you exquisite grotesque!
Half woman and half animal.

Come forth my lovely languorous Sphinx,
   And put your head upon my knee
   And let me stroke your throat and see
Your body spotted like the Lynx!

—OSCAR WILDE

I have studied many philosophers and many cats. The wisdom of cats is infinitely superior.

—HIPPOLYTE TAINE

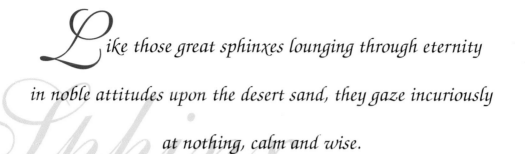

Like those great sphinxes lounging through eternity

in noble attitudes upon the desert sand, they gaze incuriously

at nothing, calm and wise.

—CHARLES BAUDELAIRE

Of all animals, he alone attains
to the Contemplative Life.
He regards the wheel
of existence from
without, like the Buddha.

—ANDREW LANG

A CLOWDER OF CATS

Unlike *Homo sapiens, Felis sylvestris* doesn't often gather in groups, generally preferring to be solitary. Regardless, the English language contains a number of colorful terms which refer to a crowd of felines, the most common being "clowder." Others include "clutter," from which "clowder" may be derived; "dout" and "destruction," which are usually used in describing wild cats; and "glaring," probably an allusion to cats' iridescent eyes. There is even a word for a bunch of kittens: "kendle," sometimes spelled "kyndyll" or "kindle."

We have cats the way most people have mice.

—JAMES THURBER

Although the cats have long lived together under the same roof . . . [they] take fiendish delight in scaring and chasing each other. . . . These disagreements do not seem serious, but more on the order of cheap thrills.

—DAVID LOVE

To a Cat

Stately, kindly, lordly friend
Condescend
Here to sit by me, and turn
Glorious eyes that smile and burn,
Golden eyes, love's lustrous meed,
On the golden page I read.

All your wondrous wealth of hair,
Dark and fair,
Silken-shaggy, soft and bright
As the clouds and beams of night,
Pays my reverent hand's caress
Back with friendlier gentleness.

Dogs may fawn on all and some
As they come;
You, a friend of loftier mind,
Answer friends alone in kind;
Just your foot upon my hand
Softly bids it understand.

—ALGERNON SWINBURNE
[excerpt]

Dear creature by the fire a-purr,
  Strange idol eminently bland,
Miraculous puss! As o'er your fur
  I trail a negligible hand,

And gaze into your gazing eyes,
  And wonder in a demi-dream
What mystery it is that lies
  Behind those slits that glare and gleam . . .

—LYTTON STRACHEY

Purrrrrrrrrr

The Murmur of Serenity

The soft hum of a cat's purr is the reassuring sound of contentment. Nursing kittens begin to purr at the age of one week, signaling that all is well; a mother cat, in turn, purrs for her litter, calming them and conveying the same sense of well-being. Purring cats soothe humans as well; there's nothing quite as relaxing and enchanting as a soft, warm cat purring in your lap.

Little Motors

Adult cats offer different types of purrs under different circumstances. The common, smooth purr, of course, generally means that the cat is contented. But a short, staccato purr may be a sort of commentary, while a very deep, loud purr can indicate distress or even pain. Cats usually stop purring while hunting, when they encounter a strange cat, and while playing with catnip. And though domestic cats are able to purr continuously—as they both inhale and exhale—big cats like lions and tigers can only generate the sound when breathing outward.

When the mouse laughs at the cat, there is a hole nearby.

NIGERIAN PROVERB

The clever cat eats cheese

and breathes down rat

holes with baited breath.

—W. C. FIELDS

A mouse in the paws is worth two in the pantry.

—LOUIS WAIN

A mouse

How silently and with what a light tread do cats creep up to birds! How stealthily they watch their chance to leap out on tiny mice!

—PLINY THE YOUNGER

It is better to feed one cat than many mice.

NORWEGIAN PROVERB

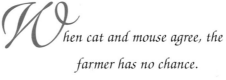

When cat and mouse agree, the

farmer has no chance.

ENGLISH PROVERB

Let us take a cat, and foster him well with milk
And tender flesh, and make his couch of silk,
And let him see a mouse go by the wall,
Anon he waveth milk, and flesh, and all,
And every dainty which is in that house,
Such appetite hath he to eat a mouse.

—GEOFFREY CHAUCER

A cat is a lion to a mouse.

ALBANIAN PROVERB

The Kitten and the Falling Leaves

See the Kitten on the wall,
Sporting with the leaves that fall,
Withered leaves—one—two—and three—
From the lofty elder tree!
Through the calm and frosty air
Of this morning bright and fair,
Eddying round and round they sink
Softly, slowly: one might think,
From the motions that are made,
Every little leaf conveyed
Sylph or Faery hither tending,—
To this lower world descending,
Each invisible and mute,
In his wavering parachute.
—But the kitten, how she starts,
Crouches, stretches, paws and darts!
First at one, and then its fellow,
Just as light, and just as yellow;
There are many now—now one—
Now they stop and there are none.
What intenseness of desire
In her upward eye of fire!
With a tiger-leap half-way,
Now she meets the coming prey,
Lets it go as fast, and then
Has it in her power again . . .

—WILLIAM WORDSWORTH

The smallest feline is a masterpiece.
—LEONARDO DA VINCI

Kitten

No matter how much cats fight, there always seem to be plenty of kittens.
—ABRAHAM LINCOLN

Young kittens assume that all other animals are cats, approach them with jaunty friendliness, and invite them to play.
—MURIEL BEADLE

An ordinary kitten will ask more questions than any five-year-old boy.
—CARL VAN VECHTEN

A kitten is the most irresistible comedian in the world. Its wide-open eyes gleam with wonder and mirth, it darts madly at nothing at all, and then, as though suddenly checked in the pursuit, prances sideways on its hind legs with ridiculous agility and zeal.

—AGNES REPPLIER

A kitten is so flexible that she is almost double; the hind part is equivalent to another kitten with which the forepart plays. She does not discover that her tail belongs to her until you tread on it.

—HENRY DAVID THOREAU

Nothing falls asleep

quite so easily as a cat.

—DESMOND MORRIS

A Cat

Philosopher and comrade, not for thee
The fond and foolish love which binds the dog;
Only a quiet sympathy which sees
Through all my faults and bears with them awhile.
Be lenient still, and have some faith in me,
Gentlest of skeptics, sleepiest of friends.

—JULES LEMAÎTRE

A little drowsing cat is an image of perfect beatitude.

—JULES CHAMPFLEURY

One of the ways in which cats show happiness is by sleeping.

—Cleveland Amory

Cats are rather delicate creatures

and they are subject to a good many

ailments, but I never heard of one

who suffered from insomnia.

—Joseph Wood Krutch

As to Sagacity, I should say that his judgment respecting the warmest place and the softest cushion in a room is infallible.

—Thomas Henry Huxley

The Four-Penny Cat

LITTLE LESSONS IN HISTORY

THEN

In ancient Egypt, cats were highly respected creatures, sometimes venerated as gods, and killing one was considered punishable by death. Somewhat later, in the tenth century A.D., Prince Howell the Good of Wales issued a more complicated set of regulations pertaining to cats, setting the price of a newborn kitten at one penny, a kitten with proven hunting abilities at twopence, and a fully grown mouser at four pence (the cost of a lamb). A person who killed a cat was compelled to compensate its owner with as much wheat as could cover the cat when held by its tail, nose on the ground. There were also specific fines for endangering a cat's life, wounding a cat, and not taking proper care of a cat.

NOW

In twentieth-century California, Governor Ronald Reagan signed into law a bill making it illegal to kick cats (under certain circumstances). Perhaps the most well-known cat legislation—An Act to Provide Protection to Insectivorous Birds by Restraining Cats—is famous not for its content, but for its veto. In a letter from 1949 explaining his rejection of this obviously pointless bill, Governor Adlai E. Stevenson wrote, "It is in the nature of cats to do a certain amount of roaming . . . The State of Illinois . . . already [has] enough to do without trying to control feline delinquency."

She Sights a Bird

She sights a bird—she chuckles—
She flattens—then she crawls—
She runs without the look of feet—
Her eyes increase to Balls—

Her Jaws stir—twitching—hungry—
Her Teeth can hardly stand—
She leaps, but Robin leaped the first—
Ah, Pussy, of the Sand

The Hopes so juicy ripening—
You almost bathed your tongue—
When Bliss disclosed a hundred Toes—
And fled with every one—

—EMILY DICKINSON

Afrikaans: katse Albanian: mace Arabic: kitte **Armenian: gatz** Basque: catua

DUTCH: KAT FINNISH: KISSA French: chat GERMAN: KATZE

Icelandic: köttur Indonesian: kucing ITALIAN: GATTO Japanese: neko KIKU

Malay: kucing MALTESE: QATT n: gurbah Polish: kot POR

macka Sicilian: ga Swedish: katt Taga

Welsh: kath YIDDIS tse Albanian: ne

CONGO: BUDI Czech: CH: KAT FINNI

chatul **HINDI: BILLY** HUNGAR ttur Indonesian: ku

maaw Latin: felis Latvian: kakis Malay: kucing MALTESE: QATTUS Mohawk

Romanian: pisica Russian: koshka Serbo-Croatian and Slovak: ma

TAHITIAN: MIMI Tibetan: shimi Turkish: kedi VIETNAMESE: MÈO

gatz Basque: catua BULGARIAN: KOTKI Chinese: mao CO

eek: ga'ta Hawaiian: popoki Hebrew: chatul HI

BAKA Korean: koyangi Laotian: maau

an: gurbah Polish: kot PORTUGU

ma ATO Swahili: paka Swedish: katt Tag

THE INTERNATIONAL CAT

Famous cat lovers: Marie Antoinette, Cleopatra, Mark Twain, Theodore Roosevelt, T. S. Eliot, Yoko Ono, Tennessee Williams, Gloria Steinem, Charles de Gaulle.

It is illegal for a cat to drink beer in Natchez, Mississippi.

The world's fattest domestic feline: Himmy, a resident of Australia who, in 1982, weighed in at a hefty 45 pounds, 10 ounces.

Cats, like people, are either right- or left-handed.

Famous cat haters: Julius Caesar, Alexander the Great, Napolean Bonaparte, Johannes Brahms, James Boswell, Adolph Hitler, Dwight D. Eisenhower.

When Edward Lear (the author of The Owl and the Pussy-Cat) decided to build a new house, he had it designed to be identical to his old one so his cat, Foss, would not be annoyed by the move.

Cats can donate blood to other members of their species.

The cat is the only domestic animal that is not mentioned in the Bible.

The Latin word for puppy is catellus.

The Cat and the Fox

One day, a fox was boasting to a cat about how clever he was. "Why, I know of a hundred different ways to escape my enemies," he claimed.

"That is truly remarkable," said the cat. "Alas, I have only one method of escaping my enemies, though it works fairly well for me. Will you teach me some of yours?"

"Well, pehaps one day when I'm not busy, I'll teach you some of the easier ones," said the fox.

In the next moment, a pack of barking dogs could be heard coming toward them in the forest. In the wink of an eye the cat scampered up a tree and hid among the leaves. "This is the only trick I know to escape the hounds," she called down to the fox. "but it usually serves me well. Which trick are you going to use?"

The fox sat and thought about his best means of escape. He went over each method in his head, weighing the pros and cons. The hounds drew closer and closer, but the fox didn't want to make the wrong choice.

Finally, he decided to make a run for it. But it was already too late, and before he could start, the dogs were upon him.

MORAL
One good plan that works is better than a hundred doubtful ones.

—AESOP'S FABLES

The Nature of Friendship

To gain the friendship of a cat is not an easy thing. It is a philosophic, well-regulated, tranquil animal, a creature of habit and a lover of order and cleanliness. It does not give its affections indiscriminately. It will consent to be your friend if you are worthy of the honor, but it will not be your slave. With all its affection, it preserves its freedom of judgment, and it will not do anything for you which it considers unreasonable; but once it has given its love, what absolute confidence, what fidelity of affection! It will make itself the companion of your hours of work, of loneliness, or of sadness. It will lie the whole evening on your knee, purring and happy in your society, and leaving the company of creatures of its own kind to be with you. In vain the sound of caterwauling reverberates from the house-tops, inviting it to one of those cats' evening parties where essence of red-herring takes the place of tea. It will not be tempted, but continues to keep its vigil with you. If you put it down it climbs up again quickly, with a sort of crooning noise, which is like a gentle reproach. Sometimes, when seated in front of you, it gazes at you with such soft, melting eyes, such a human and caressing look, that you are almost awed, for it seems impossible that reason can be absent from it.

—THÉOPHILE GAUTIER

'Twas that reviving herb, that Spicy Weed,
The Cat-Nip. Tho' tis good in time of need,
Ah, feed upon it lightly, for who knows
To what unlovely antics it may lead.

—OLIVER HEREFORD

I have noticed that what cats most appreciate in a

human being is not the ability to produce food, which they take for

granted—but his or her entertainment value.

—GEOFFREY HOUSEHOLD

Meow, Miaow, Mieaou

⸺◈⸺

The English lexicon recognizes at least fifteen different spellings of the word meow, including "mieaou," one of the few words in the language which contains all five vowels. This amazing multiplicity is an apt comment on the equally astonishing range of cat language.

In 1944, an American scientist divided feline vocalizations into three categories: murmurs, happy purrlike sounds created with a closed mouth; calls, variations on "meow," begun with an open mouth and completed with the mouth closing; and cries, made with the mouth entirely open. A controversial study conducted in France found that catspeak contains over six hundred different "words."

Cats speak a subtle language
in which few sounds carry many meanings, depending
on how they are sung and purred.

—VAL SCHAFFNER

Long Live the Cat!

The cat has nine lives—three for playing,

three for straying, three for staying.

—English saying

In the blithe days of honeymoon
With Kate's allurements smitten,
I lov'd her late, I lov'd her soon,
And called her dearest kitten.

But now my kitten's grown a cat,
And cross like other wives,
O! by my soul, my honest Mat,
I fear she has nine lives.

—James Boswell

There is no more intrepid explorer than a kitten.

—JULES CHAMPFLEURY